The Snatcher

Anthony McGowan ■ Jonatronix

Chapter 1 – NICE ninjas

Do you want the chance to join an elite group of young scientists? We are looking for the next generation of inventors, researchers and innovators.

Ant had been walking along the corridor when the NICE logo on the school noticeboard hooked him like a trout caught with a fly. It was the rest of the message that reeled him in, though.

Why not come along next Thursday with your greatest invention. Our panel of experts will pick the winner, who will then be invited to join the NICE Science Ninjas!

"I'd do anything to win that competition and join NICE as a *real* scientist," Ant murmured to himself. He was so engrossed he didn't see the enormous figure looming up behind him.

It was Jimmy McCoy, chewing gum as usual, even though it was banned in school and he didn't even like it – he just enjoyed breaking the rules. Jimmy was the biggest boy in Greenville school. He looked like an adolescent ogre and had the attitude to match.

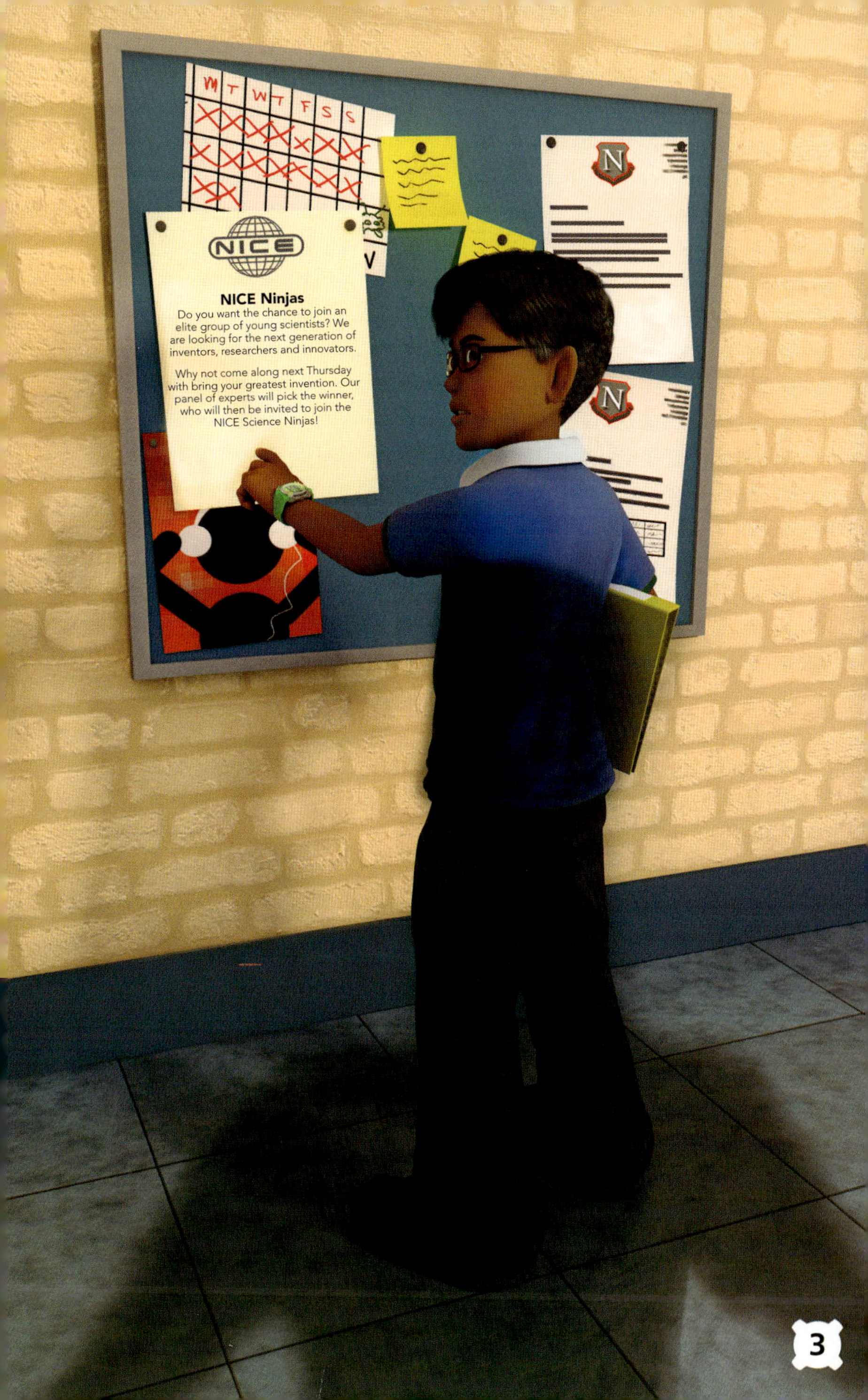
M T W T F S S
NICE
NICE Ninjas
Do you want the chance to join an elite group of young scientists? We are looking for the next generation of inventors, researchers and innovators.
Why not come along next Thursday with bring your greatest invention. Our panel of experts will pick the winner, who will then be invited to join the NICE Science Ninjas!
N
N

"You – a Ninja?" Jimmy sneered. "Let's see your moves then." He gave Ant a shove that sent him sprawling against the wall.

Jimmy guffawed, his laughter like the braying of a donkey.

"Leave him alone!" A clear, sharp voice rang out down the corridor.

Ant looked up with relief to see Cat stalking along the corridor, her anger bubbling just below the surface like a kettle about to boil; Ant was very pleased she was on his side.

Even though Jimmy McCoy was twice her size, he was a little afraid of Cat – although, of course, he'd never admit it – and so, even before Max and Tiger arrived to back her up, Jimmy had already begun to edge away.

As he left, he threatened Ant, "One of these days I'm going to feed that pet hamster of yours to Gripper."

Jimmy's dog, Gripper, was infamous – even though nobody had ever actually seen him, rumour had it he looked like he was assembled from the meanest parts of the most vicious dogs. In fact, it was even said that Gripper could fell a tree by chomping through the trunk with his razor-sharp teeth.

Everyone was too scared to go anywhere near Jimmy and his dog, especially as Jimmy relished saying things like, "He's as big as a horse, you know?" or "He's as strong as a bull!" or "He'll have your leg off as soon as look at you!"

Even though no one really believed anything Jimmy said, almost everyone had heard Gripper barking and growling and snarling behind the fence in Jimmy's garden and they weren't willing to take the risk.

"Thanks, Cat," said Ant.

"Jimmy's a brute and a bully," said Cat. "Just ignore him."

Ant nodded but he was still feeling a bit shaky. He was pretty sure Jimmy was bluffing, absolutely positive … but, well, Ant had an active imagination. He chased away the images and resolved to keep a close eye on his hamster, just in case.

Max and Tiger headed towards them. "What's this about a science competition?" asked Max, pointing to the board.

"Dani mentioned it to me a while ago," replied Ant. "She's been trying to persuade me to enter."

"You should," said Tiger. "You're definitely the brainiest kid in this school. Hey, you might just be the brainiest kid in *any* school!"

"Thanks, Tiger," Ant replied. "The trouble is it's open to young scientists up to the age of 18. I doubt I'd stand much of a chance against the older entrants."

"Don't give up before you've even tried, Ant," said Max encouragingly. "Just have a go. You never know what might happen."

Ant looked thoughtful. He didn't mention it to the others but he did, in fact, have an inkling of an idea. The trouble was that it was potentially quite risky. Dangerous, in fact. However, he knew that if he wanted to win, and become a NICE Science Ninja, it would mean throwing caution to the wind.

Chapter 2 – Secret Ant

For the next week, the others hardly saw Ant. Whenever Tiger went round to his house, Ant's mum said he was out or busy with his homework. At school, he hurried to his lessons, barely pausing to say hello and when the others asked him if anything was wrong, Ant would simply reply "No, I'm fine!" or "Just a bit busy."

By the end of the week, Max, Cat and Tiger had had enough. On Saturday morning, they gathered outside Ant's house; they wanted answers. Eventually, Ant appeared, carrying a sports bag and glancing around furtively.

"What are *you* doing here?" Ant said, sounding shocked and a bit guilty.

"We want to know what's going on, Ant," demanded Tiger.

Cat gave Tiger a cross look. "We're *worried* about you, Ant. We've hardly seen you lately."

Ant looked at the floor. "I'm sorry. It's just … I'm working on something." He paused. "It's for the science competition."

"That's brilliant – why didn't you tell us?" asked Max.

"Well, I didn't know if you'd approve," said Ant sheepishly. "You see, I've discovered a small amount of an interesting substance inside one of Dr X's damaged X-bots. It seems to be an unusual alloy that reacts with water, generating minute explosions. If I can make it power a miniature engine, I'm *convinced* this will be the next big thing in green energy," continued Ant growing increasingly excited. "I'm getting there but I've only got four days left before the competition so there's no time to waste."

"With that, Ant hurried off. Cat turned to the others, a look of concern on her face. "Do you think he should be using *that* technology?"

"Well, it's for a NICE competition so it should be OK, shouldn't it?" replied Tiger.

"I suppose," agreed Max. "It's probably best if we leave him to it. I'm sure he won't take risks."

For the next four days, Ant worked tirelessly on his project. Only one thing spoiled the week for him: whenever he came across Jimmy McCoy, the bully, he would gnash his teeth.

"Why's he doing that?" asked Tiger, when he saw him.

"He's pretending to be Gripper," Ant replied.

Cat gave Jimmy a stern look – she might actually have growled – and he scuttled away.

Chapter 3 – A night to remember

On Thursday evening, NICE was buzzing with excitement, its largest conference room alive with nervous chatter. Max, Cat and Tiger were in the front row, keen to support Ant. They were surprised to see Jimmy McCoy sitting near them, though it was clear he hadn't come of his own accord; his mother was sitting right next to him. Jimmy looked bored and when Jimmy got bored that usually meant only one thing – trouble.

At the front of the room stood the four contestants, their inventions and experiments set up in front of them. The judging panel, including Dani, waited patiently to their left.

Ant tried to hide his nerves but he wasn't the only one feeling nervous: most of the young scientists looked apprehensive. Except, that is, for one boy – Rodney Grape. He was wearing a neat suit and a tie and he looked as though he already worked for NICE. Ant had heard about Rodney. In fact, he was something of a science hero of Ant's; he'd already been moved up a year in school and was considered an incredibly gifted young scientist. Ant knew Rodney would be hard, if not impossible, to beat.

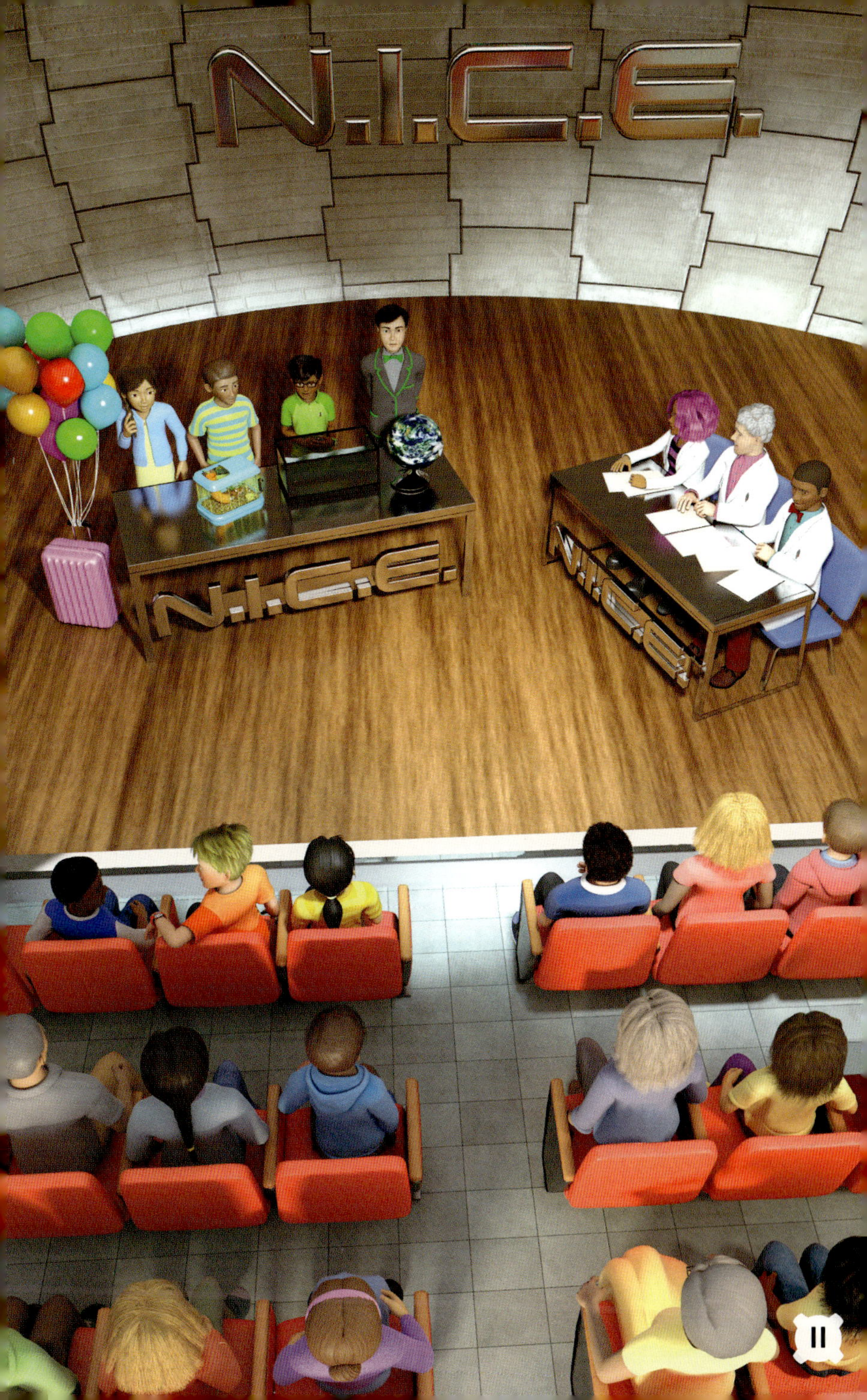
N.I.C.E.
N.I.C.E.

The audience fell silent and, with a nod from the judges, the contest began. The first demonstration was by a girl who had designed a suitcase attached to helium-filled balloons so that it weighed almost nothing. She hadn't actually *made* the suitcase and her diagrams indicated that she'd need at least a thousand balloons to actually make it work.

Next was a boy who had devised a way of translating animal noises into human words. He held a little microphone next to his pet rat's mouth, which picked up the squeaks it made. A small speaker then broadcast the translation: "I want cheese. I want cheese. I want cheese."

An expectant chatter spread around the room as the third contestant stepped forward. Rodney Grape paused, waiting for silence, and then began his presentation. In front of him stood a model of the Earth with a small rocket attached to a metal track which was orbiting the earth.

"This is my design for my Spaceliner RG1000," declared Rodney confidently. "It will be the next big thing in space travel, no doubt about it!"

“That’s not bad,” whispered Tiger, “but it’ll never beat Ant’s invention.”

Then Rodney Grape did something that astonished them all: he removed the rocket track and started the engine again. Still, the little rocket somehow orbited the model Earth.

A huge round of applause rippled through the audience. Rodney didn’t look at all surprised by the adulation; it was clearly something he was used to.

Then came Ant’s turn. His heart was pounding. All his hard work would now be judged.

Ant had placed his model boat, with its modified outboard motor, at the centre of a tank filled with water. He added a carefully carved little figure of himself, placing it carefully on a tiny ejector seat. He planned, as his finale, to eject mini-Ant into the audience so that ‘he’ could gracefully float down on the end of a parachute.

As the audience fell quiet, Ant started the engine with a drop of water, setting off the reaction in the alloy. The boat surged across the tank at a terrific speed.

“Go Ant!” yelled Tiger, his excitement getting the better of him.

However, it soon started to go wrong. First, the boat kept careering into the sides of the glass tank. Then smoke began to billow from the engine. Smoke became sparks, sparks became flames and finally the boat smashed into the side of the glass tank and exploded like a magnificent firework.

The blast cracked the glass. The crack spread slowly, until it burst impressively, under the weight of the water, which gushed out, like a waterfall, onto the stage. At the same moment, the ejector seat was triggered, sending the mini-Ant rocketing into the ceiling, where it stuck, like an arrow in a target.

A stunned silence fell over the audience. Max, Cat and Tiger felt so sorry for their friend; they knew how bad he must be feeling.

The silence was broken by Jimmy McCoy, his raucous laughter and slow, sarcastic clapping echoing around the room.

Ant didn't wait for the verdict. Everyone knew that Rodney was the winner. He just ran out of the building and didn't stop until he was home. He climbed into bed, pulled the duvet over his head and tried to forget about the worst day of his life.

Ant's hurried exit, however, meant he missed the commotion at the very end of the competition.

While Dani was awarding first prize to a smug-looking Rodney, a desperate cry rang out: "Ratty, where's my ratty?"

It was the boy who thought he could translate his rat's squeaks into human language.

The audience soon realized what this meant and panic started to spread like wildfire.

"The rat!"

"Escaped!"

"They're filthy creatures!"

"They're flea-ridden, disease-carrying vermin!"

"Arrgghh!"

People stood on chairs or raced for the exits.

Only one person appeared to be enjoying the chaotic scene: Jimmy McCoy. He just sat there with a monstrous grin stretched across his face.

Chapter 3 – The disappearing rodents

"Cheer up, Ant," said Tiger, as the two of them walked to school the next day. Tiger had gone out of his way to collect Ant from his house. He knew from his own experience how rotten you could feel when things didn't go to plan.

Ant smiled back at him. He was trying to forget about his humiliating defeat. There would be other opportunities and, anyway, he was already part of NICE. He was a member of Team X.

As Ant and Tiger reached the school gates, they saw a small crowd gathering. At the very centre was a girl from Tiger's class, Sarah Mason. She was crying desperately as her friends tried to comfort her.

"What is it, Sarah?" asked Tiger. He liked Sarah – she always helped him when he couldn't get the numbers to quite add up in class.

"It's my hamster, Geronimo. He's disappeared!"

“I’m sure he’ll turn up,” said Tiger comfortingly. “Pickles is always going missing, isn’t he, Ant?”

Ant rolled his eyes. “All the time. Mostly he likes to hide behind the skirting boards but he usually comes out in the end, although he did hide there for a week, once!”

Sarah wailed.

“I’ll tell you what, Sarah,” said Tiger. “We’ll come round to your house after school and help you look for him. You’d be surprised how good we are at finding things.” Then Tiger whispered to Ant, “We can shrink and look in all the hard-to-reach places.”

So, after school that day, all of Team X found themselves in Sarah’s neat bedroom, complete with its empty hamster cage. The five of them looked everywhere – even the rubbish bin – but found no trace of Geronimo. However, they knew they couldn’t look properly with Sarah about – they needed to get her out of the way.

“Why don’t you wait downstairs?” said Max to Sarah. “We’ll have one last look. Maybe you could get us some juice?”

“OK,” said Sarah, still sniffing, her eyes red from crying.

As soon as Sarah had gone, Team X turned the dials on their watches and shrank to micro-size. Moving quickly, they looked under the bed and in every nook and cranny of the room. No sign. Then Tiger stepped in something. He was stuck.

"Help!" he cried. "It's got me!"

The others hurried to his side. Max was the first to start laughing. "Tiger, it's just some chewing gum."

Cat and Ant were busy helping pull Tiger off the sticky mess when they heard the thumping of Sarah's feet on the stairs.

"Quick, guys," whispered Max. "We need to grow back to normal size!"

Sarah's face was full of hope when she appeared with a tray of glasses filled with juice.

"Did you …?"

Tiger shook his head sadly. He felt terrible.

As they left Sarah's house, Cat was lost in thought. There was something significant, she was sure, about the chewing gum. She had never seen Sarah chew gum and she certainly didn't seem like the kind of girl who would just spit it out under her desk. It was looking more and more likely that there was a pet thief on the loose …

Chapter 4 – The Pickles plan

Over the next few days, the mystery deepened. Firstly, a guinea pig called Donald disappeared from its hutch. The owner was a pensioner called Harold Larwood; he'd put up wanted posters all over Greenville.

The very next day, a pair of gerbils called Ringo and Poyo were stolen. Their owner was another girl at Greenville school, Tracey Conway. When Cat tried to comfort her at break, Tracey just kept saying: "At least I've still got my little rabbit, Fluffy."

The next night, the burglar returned.

Fluffy disappeared.

There was even a report about the crime wave on the local news. The sobbing owners were all interviewed, each holding a picture of their lost pets.

Ant watched in horror. "Don't worry, Pickles. Whatever happens, I won't let them get you."

It wasn't long before almost every small pet in Greenville had been stolen. Without a single clue to go on, the police soon gave up trying to find the culprits.

Breaking News ... Greenville Pets Stolen

"It's time for Team X to do something about this," said Max. They all knew Pickles was in serious danger so had joined Ant to see what they could do.

"What's the plan, Max?" asked Tiger. "Are we going to defend Pickles to the death in an epic fight?" He was quite looking forward to solving the mystery and being a hero.

Max didn't actually have a plan but, thinking on his feet, he said, "Er, no. We're going to let the hamster-knapper knap Pickles."

"WHAT!" exclaimed Ant, "Are you serious? Oh, and 'knap' doesn't even mean that!"

But Cat smiled. "I get it. We're going to use Pickles as bait. We'll let the thief grab him, then track them back to their lair and free all the pets."

"I'm not at all happy about this!" said Ant, crossing his arms.

"Look," said Max, reasonably. "We're Team X. We've battled some of the nastiest villains in the world. Pickles will be perfectly safe."

Max, Cat and Tiger looked at Ant: it was his decision.

After a *lot* of persuasion and guarantees of Pickles' safety, Ant reluctantly agreed and that evening Team X put their plan into action.

Max, Cat and Tiger were bursting with excitement; it had been a while since they had had a real mystery to solve and this time the fate of Pickles was at stake. They had to succeed. They just had to.

Hawkwing, poised and ready, stood in the middle of Ant's bedroom.

"I don't think Dani will mind us borrowing Hawkwing, will she? It's for a good cause and I *did* try to ask her but she seemed really busy. I think she's worried the Collector is planning something."

"As long as we return it quickly, I'm sure it'll be OK," reassured Max. "Now, let's get into position."

Max and Cat shrank to micro-size and climbed into Hawkwing. Ant and Tiger shrank down to nano-size, made their way carefully into Pickles cage and hid amongst the sleeping hamster's fur.

"Er, what happens if Pickles has a scratch," asked Tiger.

"There's a spot right between his shoulder blades he can't reach," Ant answered confidently. "Let's hide there."

With everyone in place, Team X waited.

Chapter 5 – Pickles picked

Cat's eyes pinged open.

A noise.

A scratch and a rattle from outside the window. She elbowed Max. "Wake up!"

This was it.

They had deliberately left the window unlocked and there was a very convenient drainpipe leading up to it, perfect for climbing up.

The sound grew louder. Cat pointed to the window. A head appeared. It was obviously a kid – but who it was they couldn't tell; a hood disguised most of their face.

Max and Cat saw the intruder's head turn slowly from side to side, obviously making sure the coast was clear. Then, the mystery intruder pushed open the window and sprang into the room, moving with great speed and agility.

In a couple of strides, they had reached the cage. Without pausing, the thief lifted the cage door and grabbed the hamster, thrusting Pickles into their jacket pocket. They then quickly retraced their steps and disappeared.

It was all over in a matter of seconds.

"Let's go," said Max, firing up Hawkwing's engines.

"I have a feeling I know where they're heading," murmured Cat, more to herself than to Max.

By the time Max had navigated Hawkwing through the window, the thief was already mounted on a bike.

"This is going to be easy," smiled Cat. She knew that Max was a brilliant pilot and he'd have no trouble following some kid on a bike.

Then something most unexpected happened. Two rocket motors flared up at the back of the bike and it shot off down the street at a terrific speed.

"Whoah!" cried Cat. "Perhaps I was wrong …"

Max rammed the throttle and they shot forward, the force of it slamming their heads back.

The next few minutes were exhilarating. The rocket bike wove all over town, zooming down narrow alleyways and through underpasses. Max was finding it more and more difficult to keep up. Suddenly, the bike swung to the right and shot down a narrow gap between two houses. Max flung the controls sharply to the right to follow the bike, Cat clinging to the sides of her seat.

"Careful, Max," cried Cat. "Watch out!" A fox, startled by the bike in front, streaked in front of Hawkwing, a blur of red as it passed.

Max wrenched the controls back, hard, dragging the aircraft vertically up. Hawkwing shuddered as they scraped over a nearby roof, sending broken tiles smashing down on to the road.

When Max swooped back down to ground level, there was no sign of the rocket bike.

LOST PROPERTY

Char

Chapter 6 – The last stop

"We've lost them!" cried Max, annoyed with himself.

"It's OK, Max," said Cat, pressing the tracker on her watch, "I should be able to track Ant and Tiger."

"Nothing. They must be out of range," said Cat, puzzled. "Or the signal is being blocked!"

"But who would have that sort of technology?" asked Max.

"Well, who would have the technology to build that rocket bike?" replied Cat. She paused. "Actually, I think I know who the pet-knapper is *and* where they live. I've had a nagging feeling since the rat in the science competition went missing."

"You have? So who …"

"There's no time to explain" said Cat. "Just fly – I'll direct you."

A couple of minutes later, they were hovering over Jimmy McCoy's house.

"I think you're right," said Max when he saw whose house they were outside. "He was at the science competition when the rat got taken and he was *always* threatening to take Pickles."

"Don't forget the chewing gum at Sarah's house – Jimmy's always chewing gum," added Cat.

At that moment, the rocket bike arrived, confirming their suspicions.

"I'm going to enjoy turning that kid in to the police," said Cat, her mouth set hard. "He's *always* been a horrible bully."

Max looked uncertain. "It makes sense in some ways but something doesn't quite add up. I mean, how did Jimmy get his hands on the rocket bike?" he asked. "Unless he's secretly more interested in science than we thought and that was why he was at the competition. And what does he want with all the pets? It just doesn't make sense."

But that thought was left hanging in the air. The thief leaned their bike against a lamppost and vaulted over the garden fence. Even though Max and Cat were inside Hawkwing, they could hear the snarling of Jimmy's menacing dog.

"Oh no!" said Cat. "Pickles! Ant and Tiger are on him, too. The brute is going to feed him to that monster-dog of his. That's why he wants the pets! Quick, Max, fly us down there!"

Max flew Hawkwing over the fence. At last they were going to meet the notorious Gripper. Max had always pictured a cross between a Rottweiler and a pit bull. Cat imagined a huge shaggy monster, with snaggle teeth and a lolling tongue.

What they *actually* encountered was the tiniest little dog either of them had ever seen. It was the size of a large rat with floppy ears and big, round eyes.

Max let out a splutter of laughter and Cat couldn't help but say, "Aw, isn't he sweet!"

Just then, 'Jimmy' did something rather strange: he grabbed the yelping Gripper.

"You'll make a perfect pilot!" he said, shoving the tiny dog under his arm. Within seconds, he had jumped back over the garden fence.

At the same moment, a window opened and a head peeped out.

"Gripper, Gripper," cried out a bleary-eyed Jimmy McCoy. "Where are you, boy?"

"What on Earth …?" began Max.

Chapter 7 – The space programme

"So who *are* they then?" Max and Cat said together, shaking their heads in bafflement.

"Only one way to find out," said Max, once more revving Hawkwing's engines.

They flew out of the garden just in time to see the thief zoom around a corner.

For the next five minutes, Max did all he could to keep up with the twists and turns of the bike. They were soon on the outskirts of Greenville, where grand houses nestled amid their stately gardens.

Eventually, the bike slowed and drove through a large set of gates.

Max flew up to a hiding place on the roof of the house, where they would have a good vantage point.

"Now we can find out who they are and what they're up to," said Max.

The thief was in the garden, an open garage behind them, into which they disappeared, returning with a box full of complicated-looking apparatus. As Max and Cat watched, the figure began to assemble the equipment, snapping parts together. It looked a little bit like an upward slanting section of a roller coaster.

"What are they up to?" muttered Cat. They were both utterly perplexed. The hood remained pulled down over the thief's face, so they still had no idea who it was.

The thief then went back into the garage and this time emerged carrying what looked like some kind of rocket. As the shadowy form lifted up the object, the hood fell back from their face.

It revealed …

"Rodney Grape! The boy who won the science competition!" gasped Max and Cat together. Now they could see exactly what he had constructed: a larger scale version of the Spaceliner he'd won the science competition with.

Max and Cat watched as Rodney opened the top part of the Spaceliner and there, inside, were Greenville's pet-knapped pets strapped into little seats.

Two seats were empty. Rodney took Jimmy's dog, Gripper, and placed him in the pilot's seat. Then he took Pickles from his pocket and put him in the last passenger seat.

"Ready for blast off?" asked Rodney, closing the hatch. He picked up a small remote control with a timer and an oversized red button on it.

"The three-minute countdown begins!" he shouted ceremoniously.

Max and Cat looked at each other, their mouths hanging wide open.

"You don't really think he is *actually* going to blast those animals into orbit, do you?" asked Cat, horrified.

"I don't know if he *can* but I have a horrible feeling he's going to *try*," answered Max, in disbelief.

The implications of this hit home like an exploding rocket. It wasn't just the animals that were in danger.

"We've got to get them out of there. I mean, Ant and Tiger … they're still on Pickles …"

Meanwhile …
Hidden deep in Pickles' fur, Ant and Tiger were desperately trying to see what was going on.

"It's the missing pets!" said Ant. "They're all around us. But where …?"

The looming form of Ant's hero appeared above them.

"What? I … I can't believe … Oh no!" said Ant. "I have a horrible feeling we're in a scaled-up version of his Spaceliner."

Tiger gulped. "We've got to get out of here!"

At that moment, the top section of the Spaceliner was firmly clamped in place. Ant, Tiger, Pickles, Gripper and all the other animals were trapped inside.

"Come on," said Ant, who was already sliding down Pickles' neck. "We've got to get to the cockpit and take control of this thing."

Inside the passenger compartment, it was mayhem. The rats, gerbils, hamsters and rabbits were strapped into their seats but they were writhing and wriggling, squeaking and scratching – all desperate to escape.

I know how you feel, thought Ant as he and Tiger struggled forward.

Ant and Tiger grew from nano-to micro-size and pushed through the rest of the animals to get to the 'cockpit' which was actually just a small space at the front of the craft. There they found Gripper, strapped into the pilot's chair. Tiger released him and he ran to the back of the rocket, cowering in a corner. Tiger quickly jumped into the pilot's seat.

"Ant, can you figure out a way to override the auto-pilot?" asked Tiger.

"I'll try," said Ant, as he pondered the vast array of dials, switches, buttons and levers before him.

"I knew that boy was good," said Ant, struggling not to admire Rodney's skills now that he knew the truth about him.

Outside, Rodney Grape began the countdown.

"*10, 9, 8, 7*… Ignition!" cried Rodney, and the rocket engines on the back of the Spaceliner fired.

Inside, Ant thought he'd worked it out. He hit three switches and turned a dial 180 degrees.

"Nothing's happening," said Tiger. "The controls are …"

"*3-2-1* … BLAST OFF!" shouted Rodney, and the Spaceliner shot off up the launch ramp.

In Hawkwing, Max and Cat looked on in horror as the little rocket zoomed into the night sky, leaving a trail of smoke behind it.

"After them!" yelled Cat. "We might be able to help them if we can keep up!" Taking control of Hawkwing, she fired the thrusters and Hawkwing soared into the night sky.

Chapter 9 – Night flight to fright

WHOOSH! The Spaceliner flew higher and higher. Tiger panicked and began to press every button and pull every lever he could reach.

Back on the ground, Rodney was chuckling to himself as the rocket dwindled to a tiny point of light in the star-filled sky.

"I've done it!" he said triumphantly. "I've really done it!"

"Done what, dear?" came a voice from behind him. "It's late, Rodney. Come inside."

"Just a minute, Mother. I'm testing another one of my flying models. I need to perfect it before I join the Science Ninjas and …" Rodney's voice became a little less sure. "I, er, want something to show Uncle."

"Well, don't be too long," replied Rodney's mother. "And don't be too disappointed if your uncle isn't impressed with your invention. You know what a perfectionist he is."

His mother left him, saying, "five minutes, no more."

It was then that Rodney noticed that the dot of light was behaving oddly: it was weaving and wobbling. He fiddled with the controls on his remote.

"Drat," he said. "Another failure!"

The dot of light began to grow bigger. Up in the Spaceliner, Tiger had accidentally hit the right combination of buttons to take control of the craft. Unfortunately, that meant the rocket was now heading at full speed back towards Rodney's house!

"Pull up, pull up!" yelled Ant.

"It's no use, I can't control it!" Tiger cried back, his knuckles turning white as he gripped the steering wheel.

In Hawkwing, Cat yelled, "Max, we've got to do something or they're going to crash! I've got an idea. Fly as close to them as you can. I'll do the rest."

Max hit full power on the afterburners and Hawkwing surged forwards. It hovered just above the speeding Spaceliner, which was on course to crash right into Rodney's house. Cat gripped the controls. Hawkwing's legs extended and the claws uncurled.

On the ground, Rodney was frozen by the spectacle of the boomerang rocket.

"It can't be …" he murmured. "My calculations … it … it's impossible."

Rodney wanted to turn and run but he was transfixed.

Then he saw, or thought he saw, a curious bird approaching his Spaceliner. It looked like an eagle but seemed to glisten in the starlight as though it was made of metal …

Inside the rocket, Tiger was still struggling with the controls.

"It's no good, Ant," he sighed. "I can't do it."

He closed his eyes, unable to watch as they blazed towards the house.

CLANK! The rocket juddered.

"YES!" screamed Cat. "I did it!"

Hawkwing's claws were clamped around the frame of the Spaceliner but it was heavy and still firing; it was dragging Hawkwing down.

"We've got to extinguish that rocket's engine or we're all going to crash," said Cat. "I think I know what we can do, though. Head for the pond in the park."

Max swung Hawkwing away from Rodney's house, the Spaceliner dangling, gripped in its claws. As they reached the park, Max angled the nose of Hawkwing towards the pond and skilfully glided down until the Spaceliner was touching the water.

FIZZ! They heard the engine sputter as it was extinguished. Max brought the two crafts to a stop at the edge of the pond.

"Good work, Max," said Cat.

"It was your idea," replied Max. "Now, let's return these pets to their rightful owners."

Chapter 10 – Home again

"That kid is a menace to society," grumbled Tiger as they headed for NICE the next day. "We've *got* to do something about him."

"One thing's for sure," said Ant, "we can't let him become a Science Ninja. Who knows what mayhem he could cause if he got his nasty hands on the facilities at NICE? We'll have to tell Dani about him."

"I suppose so," said Max. "That does mean we'll have to tell her about our covert operations, though. I hope she's not going to be annoyed."

As Team X walked down the corridor to the NICE labs, their palms became clammy and their throats dried so that barely a whisper was uttered. They nervously opened the door to Dani's lab, wondering where to begin. However, before they had the chance to speak, Dani said, "Hey, I was just about to call you, Ant."

"You were?" gulped Ant. *She must have found out about our secret mission,* he thought, worried that this could spell the end of Team X.

"I got a message from the boy who won our science competition – Rodney Grape – you remember him?" continued Dani.

"Yeah, you could say that …"

"Well, he's done something rather strange."

"You can say that again," said Tiger, under his breath.

"He's turned down his place as a NICE Ninja."

"He has?" Ant was astonished. "Why?"

"That's the *really* odd thing," said Dani. "He just said that he'd had a better offer."

"A better offer?" asked Cat.

None of Team X could understand who or what could possibly make a better offer to any budding scientist.

Dani shook her head in wonderment. "Apparently, he's going to work with a superior scientist." She creased her brow.

"But there aren't any superior scientists," said Ant. "NICE has the best brains in the world!"

"That's what we've always thought," said Dani, shrugging, "but his loss is your gain, Ant."

"Huh?"

"This means that you get to take his place; and please don't tell me *you've* had a better offer!"

"Never!" said Ant, his smile as wide as a rocket trail in the night sky.

Meanwhile …